Other books by Author

Recipes from the Kitchens of Cosmic Pizza and Simply Delicious Pizza
(Now available on Kindle and in Paper Back)

Recipes from the Kitchen of The Chocolate Martini
(Now available on Kindle and in Paper Back)

So You Want To Open a Restaurant Expanded Addition
Includes Recipes from the Kitchens of Cosmic Pizza and Simply Delicious Pizza as
well as Recipes from the Kitchen of The Chocolate Martini into this one book
(Now available in Paper Back and Kindle)

How to Retire in Panama
(Now available on Kindle)

How to Buy and Own Land in Baja Mexico
(Now available on Kindle)

From the Inside, Florida Divorce
(Now available on Kindle and in Paper Back)

Books of Scams and Other Things
(Now available on Kindle)

About the Author

The author has owned Real Estate and Mortgage companies, 8 Restaurants, Legal Document companies in Florida, Marketing and Advertising companies, Marketing and Manufacturing companies as well as Holistic Schools.

This addition of "So You Want to Open a Restaurant" comes with additional business information and our Management spread sheets used to control our restaurants costs and profits.

Acknowledgment

I have always realized that when entering a new business arena there is someone or a few someone's that I needed to seek out to learn from. I needed a mentor or mentors!

In short - You must know when you're the Master and when you're the Student.

That is what I hope I can be for you, a Mentor!

So You Want to Open Your Own Restaurant
Table of Contents

Introduction

Let's start with a little story about ego, attitude and the expectation that others have for you and you think you have for yourself.

I was a rich man's son, well actually an adopted son, living in an upper class county outside of New York City.

I was raised at a time when being in the corporate world was king. Where being the President, CEO or Chairman was the goal. Titles were everything! You get the picture.

While on this approved path I worked in marketing and sales as well as product development and manufacturing learning from many different people.

I was let go a few times along the way and while between jobs, twice, I was given the chance to open Sandwich shops.

The first time was by a fellow worker who saw that things were not going well at a company we worked for in the Chicago area. He proposed we partner in a sandwich shop. He showed me the numbers and they were really good.

Well I couldn't see myself making sandwiches after all what would people think? My friend went ahead without me and when I checked 5 years later he had 12 shops and was doing very well. I count this as mistake number 1.

Fast forward and after 5 years working at another company in New Jersey I left because they gave me a $700 bonus on $700,000.00 of new business from a new division I opened for the owner. The net profit was $300,000. The owner had told me to trust him when we spoke of bonus money during hiring... What can I say; I didn't nail down what he meant when he said, "Trust Me". Well I was between again by choice.

Just before the above mentioned move my family fell on hard times. My father passed away, taxes and bad planning left my mother financially concerned and she asked me to help her to find a business. She had never worked while being married and had few options so a business of her own made sense.

When I asked what she had in mind she spoke of a lunch place she visited with a friend of hers, a pasta bar. I asked for the address and visited. See, I believe in studying competitors. You can learn many things just from visiting successful places. Menus give you a lot of information.

What I found was a businessperson's lunch place with 20 counter seats, 1 cook and 1 server. The equipment consisted of an 8 gas burner Pasta Stove atop a refrigerated 4 drawer prep table.

The Stove had a sink and a refrigerated open top with different sauces in each of the storage pans.
There was also a bread toaster and soda fountain.

On that day they turned the seats about every 20 minutes or in other words 60 plates an hour.

The lunch rush hour ran from 11:30 to 1:30.

The expected daily plating was 120 plates. Lunch sold for $5.00 plus drinks for $1.00 totaling $6.00.

The system was simple. The server took the order for whatever style pasta and sauce was wanted and gave the order to the cook using a circular order holder which kept the orders in a first in first out order basis.

The pasta was pre-cooked earlier in the morning, drizzled with olive oil and placed in a container in the refrigerated drawer below the stove.

Any pasta style offered on the menu was in these drawers in its own container.

As the order came in the cook opened the drawer below and took out the portion, about ¼ pound and put it in a 10 inch pan, added the sauce selected with a 4 ounce ladle and heated the order, plated the order with a piece of garlic bread and placed the written order and plate on a shelf for the server to serve to the proper seat, (each seat was numbered on the servers side of the counter).
Pretty simple on the surface but really well thought out!

So what do the numbers mean? Let's break the income down.

Since this was exploratory and for purposes of simplicity we will use a formula of 33% is food cost, 33% is rent, marketing and utilities and 34% is cost of employees.

I sat down and figured basic food cost on what I would have to pay at my local grocery store instead of making my own pasta, sauces and bread. After all we really can't do much more at this time and we are just developing a model

For example purposes, at today's prices, you can expect to pay about $1.30 for 1 pound of pasta, $3.50 for one 24 oz. jar of sauce and $2.50 for Italian bread.

Approximate cost of plating ¼ pound of pasta looks like this. Pasta equals $0.33, Sauce equals $0.88 and Bread equals $.063 giving a total cost of $1.84 for this plating plus soda cost of $0.16 or $2.00. (Ok this is an example, soda will cost more in a can or bottle.)

If we use 3 times cost to come up with a menu price we would sell our pasta and soda for $6.00. This is the same price as our study above on purpose.

Our gross for 120 plates is $720.00 per day, 5 days a week, ($3600.00), or $14400.00 every 4 weeks.
Yearly this comes to a gross of about $187,200.00. Not bad for a family business.

However if our model is correct the employees and the owner receive a total of $63,648.00, (34%) after expenses. Great income if the 2 employees are married.

In 1971 that wasn't a bad income. Mom didn't see working this hard and would have had to hire people.

Even with a smaller return as a non-working owner she didn't see it and later married her friend.

I let the concept go but it did start an Idea growing in my mind.

Shortly after my mother married. I was still looking for a new direction.

My new step brother had a sandwich shop on Waters Street in New York City, which is downtown near Wall Street, with another fully coded kitchen up stairs that wasn't being used.

He offered it to me under the best terms possible, FREE, he would even train me... Me make sandwiches? No way. Mistake number 2!

Boy was I a fool! Are you getting the picture yet? I still hadn't.

Being smart and having a good business reputation in my industry I ended up as a VP of marketing in a company grossing $150,000,000. 00. I stayed for 2 years.

I then went out and formed my own company, a Sales/ Advertising firm that included telemarketing to business and fund raising products for the Telephone Pioneers.

Now I was a President, (salesman) and no longer a line item in a corporate budget. Unfortunately I traveled for 6 to 8 months a year.

During the above mentioned travel I was taken to a restaurant by a client that reminded me of my research for my mother.

As you entered the restaurant you saw a crew of ladies making, you guessed it, Pasta.

All of the pasta was made by hand and hung to dry while waiting for orders. This was a full service restaurant complete with visual entertainment, the ladies making pasta.

Additionally, there was the wonderful aroma of fresh baked bread.

Boy did this owner know how to make you hungry and wanting pasta and bread! I never forgot that restaurant.

Time moves on.

I made a lot of money doing business while traveling those 12 years, but had no life.

Finally in 1986 divorced, burnt out and living in North California, I started over. I had no desire to do any of the things I did in the past. I wanted no STRESS.

Mendocino County in Northern California is wonderful, open and non-judgmental when it comes to how one makes money.

You are who you are and most of the time you meet people and never know their given name.

The city I lived in was small. I was the only Loan Broker and later bought the local Laundromat and about 20 acres of ocean view property. Life was good!

Somewhere in there I fell in love with a special woman and married. So I became "we".

In a small town next to where we lived was the best Pizza restaurant in the area. The owner had a branch in my town and had sold it with terms to a local couple.

Unfortunately, they had failed to pay him and he had some financial obligations he needed to pay and came to me for a loan.

I usually held land, real property as security, but I knew he was not going to be able to pay me back.
So I asked him what he had as security. I did not want to take his home.

He told me about the Pizzeria in my town that he was about to take back and I agreed to take the equipment as security, but if I did get the equipment he had to train me at his pizzeria for 1 month, which was what happened. I put the equipment in storage.

You see Enlightenment, at last, came when I realized that I could get into the restaurant business for the cost of a loan to this area restaurant owner. Complete with training. The loan was just $5000.00 and I had received so much more. I had a mentor to learn from! I was ready to listen and learn.

I worked with him in the afternoon doing prep work and in the evenings making and serving pizza for a month and was taught a lot; everything that a person needed to know when it came to a pizzeria, including making dough, sauces, and a list of suppliers etc.

After getting the equipment and storing it under my Laundromat until a location could be found I started putting together a menu that included pizza, pasta and soup and salads and tested the recipes on family.

I started looking for an ocean view location in Mendocino County, Northern California for our restaurant.
I also started the necessary cost studies for plating our dishes, (what it costs to make the food we would be serving including utilities and rent.)

Additionally, I visited many different restaurants and pizzerias within an 80 mile radius of our planned location. I believed in knowing the competition, their menu items including what they charged.

Almost 20 years from the first sandwich shop partnership offer I opened our first restaurant, Simply Delicious Pizza. 5 more Simply Delicious Pizza locations were added. Then we opened Zarducci's and later Cosmic Pizza and The Chocolate Martini. The last 2 restaurants mentioned benefited from our experience with multiple units.

I truly made a mistake by expanding Simply Delicious Pizza and had to eventually close and sell all but the first one which became Cosmic Pizza. It was a wonderful learning experience. Stay small!

Well, that's how we became "Restaurateurs".

Let's see if we can make your path to owning your own restaurant an easier experience in much less time than it took us!

I want to mention that even today you can open a restaurant with $5000 worth of equipment or even less! It all depends on the menu you create, the food style, Hamburgers require a grill and Pizza requires an oven.

Also there is nothing wrong with using "Used" equipment.

Opening Your Own Restaurant

How many people do you know, besides yourself, who say, "I'd like to open a restaurant" I'm a great cook and all my friends and family have suggested it!

I know quite a few people who have said that to me over the years after they found out that we did and without any formal training. I bet you can think of quite a few too.

So let's explore what it was like to open Cosmic Pizza. It was more than a Pizzeria. Later in the Chocolate Martini section we'll learn what it was like to open that restaurant but we'll sometimes add a comment in this section as well.

Cosmic Pizza replaced our first Simple Delicious Pizza restaurant in Mendocino County and was located in a small city of about 440 people. Many tourist attractions were in the area. Tourism was seasonal. This location was open 12 years.

Business Plan

OK, you can cook, you have recipes, you have desire and support from your family and friends... now you need a business plan, a step by step guide to get started.

If you have worked in the food industry you have some idea of what goes on in restaurants. Of course, you've eaten out and you've seen someone else's vision. It all started with a dream and a plan. There are many places to start a plan. Some might start differently than I'm about to but this is how my wife and I did it.

We both worked and our monthly budget was based on a cash only, no credit cards and only monthly bills related to things like our mortgage, business rent, utilities, food and entertainment, very basic, very simple living.

I also have a marketing and manufacturing background. Babette, my wife, had worked as the bookkeeper of Marin Fish and Poultry and owned a share as well. Marin Fish and Poultry was a wholesale distributor open to the public as well as a restaurant.

As mentioned above we obtained our equipment from a loan security deposit.

The equipment was very specific for the making of pizza. So was the training.

I've had no formal training as a chef but have always cooked and read cook books.

The equipment included assorted small ware, storage trays for dough ball storage, a small Lincoln Impinger oven, a 30 quart Hobart Mixer, A 8 foot refrigerated prep table, one reach-in 2 door refrigerator and 1 single door freezer, 2 stainless work tables, seats and tables for 20 people and a 3 compartment sink.
Later we added 4 wood picnic tables for the outside deck. I paid the equivalent of $5000 for all this equipment. It was worth over $12000.

If the equipment was purchased new the cost would be greater than $30,000.

I would only buy new equipment if I could not pick up used equipment at auction (restaurant closings sometimes create auctions so the landlord can clear their space and recoup some money from the sale of equipment), or from a used restaurant equipment supplier. Look at your local newspapers or on the internet for used restaurant equipment auctions. Even EBay has great prices.

Today the internet can and does provide some wonderful education on cooking styles, equipment use, You Tube videos and of course cooking shows and recipes. Food network has many shows that can help you. Use them!

OK, let's get down to business and basics

Here are the first 12 questions to ask yourself, (we're just focusing on necessary items you need think about).

1. What are my menu items going to be?
2. What are the approximate costs of each dish?
3. How many people will be served at each sitting?
4. How large a space will be needed to serve that many people?
5. What will be served at your restaurant and what style of plate and silverware will be needed to present those dishes, paper plates or crystal?
6. What is your décor and it relationship to the type of food you'll serve?
7. What equipment do I need to prepare our menu?
8. Will this restaurant be open for Breakfast, for Breakfast and Lunch, Lunch only, Breakfast, Lunch and Dinner or just Lunch and Dinner or just Dinner?
9. How many employees', if any, will I need besides myself and spouse?
10. Will I Cater, Deliver, have a Mobile Food Truck or Cart in addition to a prep kitchen or a fixed location restaurant?
11. Will we take over a location that wants to sell or has closed or do we build?
12. How much money do we need to open and continue to live as we are now?

Before you panic or give up your dream let me give you some important input. When I found a location for Simply Delicious Pizza, later called Cosmic Pizza, it was already coded by the Mendocino County as a food location. It already had the right type of floor and coving. It was 600 square feet.

We set up the kitchen in half the space and put 20 seats in the front with an ocean view. The build out cost, with my wife and I doing a lot of the simple stuff was less than $5000. We did use a contractor at times. (The Chocolate Martini was located in a Hotel where the restaurant failed. We took the location over and were operational in 2 weeks. State side it will take longer.)

Our Cosmic Pizza décor vision was to promote local artist, let them display their art and have live plants hanging in the windows. Some days artists would actually work in the restaurant talking to our guests.

Our menu was based on Sour Dough Pizza, Homemade Pasta, Ribs, Soup and Salads plus specials like Ravioli, Dungeness crab, Salmon, Oysters, Maine Lobster. (The menu can be found in the back of this book.)

We were open 11:45 AM to 10:00 PM for Lunch and Dinner during tourist season and from 4:00PM to 8:00PM for dinner only out of season.

We would open for school lunch delivery orders during the off season and would open to feed guests a when a local B&B had people show up after all the area restaurants had closed.
We made the B&B happy, they in turn had happy guests and we had wide support from all the B&B's in the area. They all kept our menu in their rooms with directions how to find us. (By putting ourselves out we had wonderful support and off season profits instead of losses.)

During Season we had 2 employees and ourselves, off season we worked the restaurant alone or with other family members who received dinner as pay.

Our gross was just over $200,000.00 per year for each of the 12 years we were open. Not bad income from a city of 440 people and maybe another 1500 from just outside of the city.

Our overhead or management formula was based on 25% for food cost, 25% for overhead, 25% for employees and ourselves and 25% profit.

Our menu prices were 5 plus times our food cost and adjusted whenever costs caused our margins to slip. In simpler terms our sales ran from $10,000 to $35,000 per month depending on the season with spring, summer and early fall being the best.
That's an average income of just under $17,000.00 per month from our 600 sq. foot space.

The kitchen, 300 sq. feet and seating area, 300 sq. feet were two 20'x15' rectangles. Nothing fancy about it, just plants and art.

Our cash output, our total investment to get started was $10,000! Almost 10 years later we added another 600 sq. feet for a prep kitchen and our bar, "Shipwrecked" for an additional $10,000. Start small! Stay Small!

While I did most of the build out and menu planning my wife worked. Her income and what we made at the Laundromat kept us afloat. I stopped loan brokering.

When the restaurant opened I was the "Chef" and she ran the front and bar, the Owner/Manager/ Bartender".

The "LAY OUT"

When I first laid out the kitchen I did it as if I were manufacturing a part, a straight line.

Totally wrong! You want a tight triangle work space with few steps between stations.

Everything you need to do should flow smoothly with no crossing over.

You need to go from station "A" to station "B" to station "C" to the stove or oven and from the stove or oven to serving or boxing.

Take your time and on a piece of paper plan the flow of work and flow of staff. Take as few steps as possible to make and serve your dishes.
In your mind walk the order through the process of receiving to making and serving. Once you have your leased space you will have to make some adjustments.

Use your common sense, it's really that simple. While planning and before I found lease space I did meet with some professional designers who also sold restaurant equipment. It was educational and approached from the stand point that I was going to do a full build out, but because of the quotes they gave me, very expensive, I always looked to find closed restaurant locations that had as many things we needed already installed.

Some locations were just terrible but others were in great locations. Never put a lot of money in décor build outs. You'll never get that money back! Also Do Not Borrow money for a build out or have non-working partners if you can help it.

I'm going to back up some now and review, in part, some of the 12 questions I wrote about earlier.

In each case I'm going to try and show you my answer and reasons for it. While I am here to guide you I'm doing it with my business logic not yours. You may have a very good answer or way of doing something that is totally opposite from mine. That's OK, this is your restaurant and you will need to follow your bliss... I'm just a guide or mentor. You know your financial abilities. I like doing things on a shoe string. I'm comfortable with used equipment. Just don't over stretch your finances!

Q and A for the above 12 questions

Question 1 through 12

Your location, menu and hours open will dictate what type of restaurant you will have.

Breakfast- You will need a location that has high traffic and great visibility with early openings.

Your menu will have breakfast foods, coffee and will need to be served FAST with a "To Go" counter or window.

If you choose a breakfast business you will also need to be an early riser and start prepping around 4 in the morning!

Breakfast can be quite profitable.

Lunch- As above location will effect what offerings should be made. Down town city locations need something more than Hot Dogs, Burgers and Pizza slices not to mention décor.

If you're lunch only then your prepping will start closer to 8 or 9:00. Lunch also can be very profitable.

Dinner- Location as always is important however people will travel farther and be in less of a hurry. Restaurant theme and décor become a factor in planning menu item.

If you're dinner only your prepping will start around 2:00 and depending on the number of turns of your tables and your bar business you should be quite profitable.

If you're in a tourist area you'll want to be near hotels or on the way to the tourist attraction. However business commuters will also be in the mix and must be thought of hence the FAST and "To GO "counter or window for breakfast and lunch.

If you're in a neighborhood you will need to have high density or be in a small town with little or no competition.

Any of the above combinations are just fine. When I mention the time to start "Prepping" I'm not saying that someone isn't going to be at the restaurant to get early morning deliveries or going to an early morning fish market or produce market. You will have to decide when you prep and shop.

Where ever you open your restaurant you will need superior food quality, pricing and service. You also want a strong base support from locals. Tourist season comes and goes!

I've written about fixed location restaurants but there is a growing trend toward Catering, Professional Cooks for special event hiring, Gorilla cooking events, (non-code cooking at a strange location, a social event by reservation only announced on social media), mobile units and carts.
Depending on where you live these may be options. In California I still needed a code kitchen to store and prepare food as well as clean equipment. There were commercial kitchens available to rent for such purposes.

This next topic must be discussed as it will impact your bottom line. I call it "Your Unwanted Partners".

Your Unwanted Partners

Landlord, Taxes, Government agencies, Insurance Companies and Refrigeration Repair Companies are like death... you can't avoid them!

In all honesty some of these people are wonderful and are there to help you do good business. However, not all!

Let's start with you partner the **"Landlord"**. I've had some wonderful individuals who owned property and looked for their $1.00 per square foot. They were great to work with.

I've had "Corporate Landlords" that were just plain greedy and nasty. Some had in-house people others had commercial real estate firms handling their business.

These clowns suck you dry providing as little as possible.

In California and other states there is a lease used by commercial managers that provides for what is called, Triple Net and Cam.
Triple net means that you pay for the space, the state or city and county taxes on the space, if any and the utilities.

 Also you will pay the rent. Let's say a $1.00 per square foot. So, 600 square feet of space cost $600 per month plus whatever the calculated Triple Net is. This is you minimum rent.

CAM is the additional percentage of sales the landlord wants for location, advertising and cost of staff at the location. The number I heard most often was 12% of gross sales. In reality that could be 25 to 50% of net sales. Sometimes they allowed the triple net to be deducted or to be a part of the 12%.

They enforce this by requiring you to provide a Profit and Loss statement as well as a Budget and Actual Sales report monthly, (samples will be found later in the Spread Sheet tools section). Like I said they are an Unwanted Partner.

Why do this at all, well given everything I heard about business at that location I thought I could still make a good profit and I did for a while. It changed because, someone in their management team and the furniture store next door to us felt they could both make more rent than we were paying at our location.

The landlord could break our contract, (it was in the lease on page 200 or so), and have us move out, which is what happened. They did "release us from our lease".

This happened at my Stockton location when the furniture store next door wanted more space. They got mine.

Make sure you know something about your landlord and how he does business. Ask the other tenants before you meet with the landlord.

I did have some wonderful landlords.
In the next section we'll look into how to negotiate a lease.

Taxes, depending where you live can include property, sales taxes you collect for the state and of course income taxes for both the state and federal government. Now there is "Obama Care". Stay Small!

Government agencies like the health department is really not there to hurt you they are there to protect the public.

They inspect for refrigeration temperatures on all your refrigerated devices, cleanliness as well as how the food is being handled and stored. They provide "Food Handling Training, at a price and you should be the one taking the course. Someone must have this certificate hanging on the wall. You will be given time to get the training.

Insurance Companies and their policies for people injuring themselves at your restaurant are usually something that is required by the landlord and will name the landlord protected from any law suits that may come your way. (I have some personal insight on this later.)

Workman Comp Insurance is also required by the state for employees you hire. As owner you can be exempted in most states but you may have to ask for permission.

Refrigeration Repair Companies are also an Unwanted Partner but you better find a good one. You can bet the farm that the refrigeration will go down on something at the worst possible moment. It's an unwritten law!

Have someone from a good company come and inspect what you have on a maintenance basis quarterly. They will clean the compressor area of clogging dust and prevent breakdowns. Keeping the dust from clogging the cooling system is unbelievably important.

How to negotiate a lease

Once you have decided what type of restaurant and menu you want and have found a location you like you will need a strategy outlining how you will approach the landlord.

Currently there are a lot of open spaces that once housed restaurants. When the previous tenant left chances are the landlord ended up with some equipment and has left everything in place so that a new restaurant would have a code kitchen.

Where I live now I can find at least 5 decent restaurant locations that are available to lease with just minor rework on the major highway through the city I live in. I know of many locations in Orlando and Saint Augustine Florida, wonderful tourist areas with lots and lots of traffic right now!

Tourist locations are always my first choice for a restaurant location.

Landlords want to rent their space. They would prefer to have tenants with previous business experience and deep pockets. We are going to assume that is NOT you!

You have to appear confident, look confident and dress the part. You need to ask the right questions. Questions like;

1. Do you know why the last restaurant failed?
2. If a small shopping center- Do you advertise the center?
3. If free standing- Do you maintain the property?
4. What are the stats- How much traffic passes by per hour? What hours have the greatest traffic passing by?
5. What is the rent per square foot and what does that include- trash, water, electric, restaurant equipment from the last tenant?
6. Will you help with the necessary build out and repair the A/C or Heating if need be? Will you replace the rug?

As you can see you can ask a lot of questions that reflect your need to know what the property value is to you.

The landlord can say yes or no to your request. You have nothing to lose. Say every request with a "SMILE".
The landlord now knows that while you may be new to this type of business you are a knowledgeable business person who is here to negotiate not just roll over!

The landlord will try to get as big a deposit as possible from you, (first, last, deposit to take the space down to bare walls when you leave).

If they will not reduce the deposit then request to pay some now and catch up on the deposit after you open. No one ever said "NO" to me when I asked for this kind of relief.

Your job is to argue that you need you capital to put the restaurant together not for deposits.

They will also try to build in a clause to automatically raise your rent every year by a percentage based on a local index of some kind and on automatic renewals of your lease. This is normal.

You want a 3 to 5 year lease with automatic renewals for the same amount of time, 3 to 5 years.

You also want rent to start after all repairs are done and the restaurant is open, (this is very important- you can NOT control licensing time tables or government inspections). He or she will most likely come back with a 60 to 90 day delay, so be ready to start when you sign the lease. Remember, always ask with a smile and have a sense of humor about you.

The landlord is going to demand you have a large liability insurance policy protecting you that also covers or holds him harmless. You will need to get one and a copy will need to be sent to the landlord to prove it!

(I'm going to tell you what I did and why. I'm not saying that you should do this, but this is *what I did*.

First, I was once married to a Personal Injury Law, the guy or gal who sues you when a customer trips or spills hot coffee on themselves and somehow it's YOUR fault!

These "Lawyers" work on a percentage bases, around 33% of the expected return from the law suit. They go after the INSURANCE.

Now I can tell you for a fact that the one time I received a call from a "Lawyer" who asked who my insurance carrier was and was told "I DO NOT CARRY INSURANCE" never called back.

They will not pursue a case when there is no insurance and they do not want your equipment, SERIOUSLY!

After I did what I needed to do for my lease I called and cancelled my insurance. I received my prorated first payment back.

The landlord only asks for proof of insurance once.

I also protected my personal property by placing it in a trust. Never hold property in your name. Use a trust. As I said this is how I did it.)

When signing the rental contract the landlord will require that you personally guarantee the agreement even if you are a Corporation or LLC. With your property in a trust there is nothing for anyone to come after. Go ahead and sign.

Even if you fail, the failure will not show up on your credit report unless you do a formal bankruptcy. So keep that in mind also.

Always, always remember that you need to keep your sense of humor. No matter how things look the landlord wants to have you rent the location.

Sometimes the landlord works with you and makes it easy to open. I had one in Napa California that was great and went to bat for me with the building department that did a flip on me after all the work was done and wanted a handy cap restroom in the kitchen in case I hired a person in a wheel chair to do kitchen work.

For that hiring to work I'd have to adjust all work surfaces as well. Unfortunately it just would not work out. I have a 50% service related disability going back to the Vietnam era and had to leave my own kitchen because it wasn't practical for me to work there.
So you can bet I didn't want to make any adjustments. Talk about California legal requirements.

Advertising and Marketing

Over the years I've tried Cable TV, Radio, Coupons, Flyers, "A" frame road side boards, Free "Get to Know us" Dinners for city council, local sports teams and local religious leaders, Newspapers and Free pizza give-a-ways in local bars and events. There is no question, only some of the ads and marketing events worked.

The best ad we ever did was a mixture of Newspaper and Free Pizza. Here's what we did and the results;

ONE small ad with the banner stating- "PROOF IS IN THE TASTING, FREE PIZZA, BRING A FRIEND!"
The body copy read...

As the new kid in town we want you to come to our GRANT OPENING of Simply Delicious Pizza and TAKE A TASTE of our PIZZA FREE!

Come with the family, bring a friend or more. FREE TASTE between 7:00 and 9:00PM on Thursday the 10/10/97 at 1234 Hwy 12, Oakdale, CA.

We had over 700 people show up at our grand opening and we were in the black on DAY 1! We also sold over 100 pizzas that night. We never ran another ad, didn't need to.
The second best ad was a mixture of Local Radio and Local Bi-weekly newspaper in our northern California restaurant called Simply Delicious Pizza.

It was a take on Abbott and Costello comedy skits. We ran the skit on local radio and as a cartoon showing the pizza frame by frame missing slices in the paper.

Hey Babett, is that Pizza good?
Oh Yes, It's Simply Delicious Pizza!
Hey Babett, where did you get it?
Simply Delicious Pizza!
Ok, I get it it's Simply Delicious Pizza, but where did you get it?
Simply Delicious Pizza!
Babett!
Simply Delicious Pizza, Port Rd, Point Arena, CA

Have fun and think outside the box! By the way go on line and look at Pizza Today magazine. Wonderful information!

Prepping for the Day

One of the hardest things to do in the beginning of any start up is to figure how much food to prepare every day.

It's hard even for established restaurants however since you're open as a business what is not used today could be used tomorrow.

That is a good reason to make a bit more than you think you might use today as long as it stores well. Eventually you will feel comfortable prepping for multiple days.

When you are cooking for family and friends you prepare food in advance and store it until your guests arrive.

Some of the meal, a roast or bird, might be cooking and nearly done when guests arrive. If you have some food left over you store it for family lunch tomorrow. So let's adjust our family party thinking to that of restaurant prepping.

You want to make as many things as possible before you open each day. Things like sauces, salads, roasts, pasta and dough. You get the idea. Also partially prepare your appetizers, main dishes and desserts.

Prepping allows you to cook and serve smoothly and fast.

First some assumptions, our name is Cosmic Pizza so we expect pizza will be a big seller. We used sour dough which means that the dough gets sourer every day it is kept in the refrigerator. We could store a batch of 90 dough balls for up to 10 days and then make bread sticks with what was left, no waste.

Making dough balls is fast and easy and we used a first in first out program. We dated all stored foods. So should you.

Since we had other foods on the menu this is what we did.
When we made fresh pasta from scratch and after it dried some but not completely, we would weigh out a quarter pound and then Ziploc bagged it and put it in the freezer. Since we made 5 pounds at a time we had 20 orders in the freezer.

When we took an order for pasta we would drop the portion out of the storage bag and into boiling water for 3 to 5 minutes and then place the pasta in a 10 inch fry pan with the proper sauce for a minute and plate and serve.

Ravioli was also made fresh and portioned out and frozen. Again when ordered the portion storage bag was emptied into boiling water.

The ravioli would float when ready, about 5 minutes. Pasta dishes were easy and ready to be served with the meal.

Pizza and Pasta dishes are very profitable and had a prominent place in our menu. We had meat, shell fish and vegetable pizza and pasta dishes and sauces, (see menus).

Our Ribs were oven baked at 325 degrees for up to 2 hours. We separated each rib prior to cooking and marinating. It made them a finger food with very little mess and ready to eat. Women loved them.

After cooking 2 slabs we portioned them for an appetizer or a main dish in storage bags and refrigerated the portions until ordered. They were then re-sauced microwaved for 3 minutes to reheat them and served.
They were great and we even had a famous BBQ judge from the Texas, Kansas and Missouri contest circuit who gave us great ratings for our ribs. (This was at the Chocolate Martini and you'll find his Trip Advisor comments in the back pages of this book. It was the same recipe we used at Cosmic Pizza.)

I hope you're getting the picture. We developed a menu that let us prep our foods so that there was as little waste as possible and one that allowed us to do less guessing.

We worked at serving quickly and the quality and consistency was top shelf.

We used reach-in refrigeration and freezers to our advantage. We also accepted that some days we would run out of menu items.

A "High Class" problem, we sold out, which was great!

Foods like fresh chicken, ribs, chopped meat, fish, live crab and live lobster require proper temperature storage like all foods, which is below 41 degrees and must be used quickly, so we ordered a limited amount.

Live food like crab and lobster were kept in refrigerators in storage boxes with ice.

Live crab and fresh caught Salmon was available fresh from the sea seasonally. Cosmic Pizza, (the old Simply Delicious Pizza), restaurant was located on a working fishing wharf and we bought directly from the fishermen. We always order limited portions of live and fresh Sea foods.

We would prepare any fresh food that was not served within 24 hours as an appetizer or we'd use Crab or Salmon as ravioli filler or a part of a Corn and Potato chowder. We would make Crab, Shrimp or Salmon cakes as well.

We would do local radio ads 2 days before we received live Lobster. We never ordered more than 24 at a time. I love Lobster boiled or grilled and any leftover Lobsters that didn't become appetizers found their way into bisque soup, pizza, salads or diablo.

Other items on our menu like oysters were bought by the case, shucked and frozen. We called the dish Smugglers Oysters. They were prepared with fresh chopped garlic and some parmesan cheese, all 6 or 12 were then placed on a metal tray frozen and then went 6 minutes thru the pizza oven. The oysters were cooked just right, Delicious!

Located on the ocean almost demanded that we served a lot of sea food but as a family restaurant we used pizza and pasta as our profit items and had adult foods so that parents would love to come to us. Food for the kids, food for adults too!

Product was always fresh and purchased by the case at least once a week. Our inventory ran at about $2500 per week. (The Spread Sheet section will show you our control forms)

We prepped produce daily and if we were short could prep on the fly. However, it was always best to over prep on weekends when we would get really busy.

Oh, we tried using distributors but found that our local super market had a better grade produce and would allow us to order cases from them at a great price. Talk to your local markets!

So when you design your menu, think about what is necessary to pre-make so that you can serve up to the number of seats you have, smoothly. Remember to plan for takeout customers as well including takeout boxes.

Once you start and have more than one seating simply adjust you prep quantity.

Soup and salad should be pre-made and ready to serve from a hot pot by your staff. Simple really, use your common sense, be ready to serve people as you like to be served.

Don't be afraid to use commercially prepared soups like Campbell Mushroom or Potato Soup as a base to add fresh ingredients too. Alessi Tuscan Bean Soup is also a good base.

Plating as an Art

Food is a visual as well as a taste and aroma experience.

A piece of meat, potato and veggie on a plate is pretty bland. However, if you add a special sauce or a flower or use a few small red potatoes fried and slightly smashed with a drizzle of butter and some green garnish, the whole presentation changes to a culinary experience to be remembered and one to tell friends about. Word of mouth counts BIG TIME. It's the best form of advertising.

By including our menus and recipes with this book we are giving you a "road map" to guide you in your thinking about plating dishes as well as the cost of the plating those dishes. Use or recipes they will help you develop your menu.

One of the biggest problems I had in Panama at the Chocolate Martini was how to present white rice in an interesting way.

We used white rice a lot because potatoes were very expensive and not always available and the locally grown starchy root vegetables were rather bland.

The answer was surprisingly simple and added color and taste to the meal, "Roasted Sweet Red Peppers" with the skin removed and then puréed in a blender.

By adding different herbs and seasonings to the pureed pepper we could bring our sauce flavors in tune with the main dish and have a wonderful white rice presentation.

The placement of items on the menu is as important as "Plating".

The eye looks first to the right side then the left. Next time you go out to eat see where your eye is drawn. Place your most profitable dishes in this location.

Included in this book you will find examples of our Spread Sheet cost control system tools. It helped us do costing and retail pricing. It's simply our approach to breaking down costs of the foods we used to make our dishes to usable costs per ounces.

It also helped us develop selling prices and overhead controls.

The whole restaurant and everything in it is an "Art Form" and you expressing yourself.

Bring all of it together even if it takes a bit of effort. The time and effort can make you a wonderful success. Watch your costs and enjoy your art form.

Be consistent in your message as to who you are, what your image is. Stay on message!

Give Yourself Time

Hey, all things take time. Take your time and plan out as much as you can but stay flexible.

Pick you name to reflect your style of food. Pick your vendors carefully because they can make or break you.

Pick your location, be it mobile or traditional for the best traffic or tourist population. Listen to your critics but listen with the ear of a professional. Not everything being said is important or has meaning when considered looking at the whole.

We all have a need to be validated. Asking family and friends what they think really doesn't make sense unless they have been in the restaurant business as owners.

You're going to ask anyway so remember it is easier to give negative feedback than positive. Also all people like to talk so while you're in the planning stage don't give specific details as to locations you're looking at or pricing or even the theme. It might get back to someone who is also looking at the same space and give them the push to move on it before you're ready.

Of course you can say, "I'm thinking about this or that". Stay vague.

When you have a feel for what you want in your menu start looking at other restaurant menus in the area.
See what they offer, what they charge and how they present plates. Also how, where and what they advertise in their effort to find customers. You have to pay attention to their prices and be completive, but don't give away the shop. Have confidence in yourself and menu!

As you grow you'll begin hiring, remember the "Help" need to be supervised and appreciated.

I can't tell you enough how important it is to have the "Help" see you take inventory, count your cash and run your bar. Cash and food will walk out the door if you don't.

If you don't show how important service and quality are and that the "Guest" is always right then your staff won't either. Standardize your dress code so that guests can see who works at your restaurant. Dress codes set up a bit of work place pride even if it's a tee shirt with your name on it or a vest with a name tag on it.

Always compliment the "Staff" in private when they have to put up with some fool and have kept their cool.

"Staff" sometimes makes a mistake or to. Have your conversation in private and always away from the "Guests" eyes and ears. Use the time to "Teach" not "Chastise" your employee.

The "Guests", in the restaurant are watching and will support you when you are polite and your business will grow. Show temper and everyone will talk about it, negatively.

When it comes to the food service and the food itself, you want the best quality available, consistently.

Making the Salads, Soups and Main Dishes look and taste better than your competition will build your reputation.

CONSISTANCY in service, food quality and appearance from day to day, week to week and month to month are a must and will help you keep your reputation.

Never forget that. Reputation is everything. You and the staff must never forget that!

One bad day can have a huge impact on your business.

If you want to change something on the menu because it isn't selling well develop a daily special from that food category, something new, and try it as a "Special" before you remove the item. Let your "Guest" make the final decision by ordering the special or the menu item.

As an example, if BBQ Wings are not selling then try Thai Chicken Satay and peanut sauce. Keep the food selling price and costs the same if possible. If the chicken satay sells well change the menu and remove the wings.

A Final Note

Restaurants are profitable, fun, but a lot of work. The food industry somehow fulfills something special within us.

Maybe it's the gratification of being appreciated or thought of as a special place in someone's memory.

Once you've been in the food industry, you almost always stay in the business. It becomes a PASSION!

With that said "Experience" is what teaches you. Take the first step and start planning your dream today.

If my wife and I were to open a restaurant today we would keep it simple. I would be the chef and handle the kitchen perhaps with someone to help prep and or do cleanup.

My wife would handle the front as she always has.

The restaurant would be small with no more than 4 - 4tops, (4 tables each seating 4 people for a total of 16 people per seating), 2 seating's per night, 3 nights per week, by reservation only; the menu price would be all inclusive except for wine or drinks.

Our "Guests" would be required to select from 1 of 4 categories- Meat, Shell Fish, Fish or Foul when making reservations.

Always have some extra of each selection so a guest can make a change or if the person making the reservation didn't know that their guest couldn't eat what was preordered. (Also, you might have an open table and someone walks in without reservation, be prepared!)

The multi course meal would be at least 5 courses served one course at a time. (Both menus found at the end of this book reflect some of the menu items we would think about serving).

This approach allows for simplicity in the kitchen prepping and simple serving, one table at a time. It would be a meal to remember and talked about with family and friends.

Perhaps it would have a theme depending on time of year, the availability of seasonal foods, an anniversary, holiday or birthday... King Louis birthday party or Jefferson's party for George Washington!

Most likely it would be just an intimate dinner with quiet music sung by Tony B or Frank or Spanish classical guitar in the background.

Of course we might just make Pizza and Pasta!

Our active days are over but the above would make a wonderful restaurant for someone to open. We'd go!

Pizza University

My wife and I are retired now but when we were active and expanding we created Pizza University to train staff.

We were also getting ready for franchising and wanted a place to help train franchisee.

Here is a short introduction to the concept of Pizza University, complete with course outline. This section will help answer some of your unanswered questions to what we presented here in this guide.

Feel free to contact us if you have anything you'd like clarified. (mickeyg61@hotmail.com)

Ok, what is Pizza University?

Very few of us actually woke up one morning and said….Hey! I'm going to open a pizza place today.

More often circumstance brought us into the industry and some of us stayed. We were trained on the job.

Before we begin let's simply state that there is no question that franchises have been very successful and will probably always attract individuals like you and I who want to run our own lives and have professional help along the way.

Today, however, people are looking for something more from the places they patronize. They want the owner there, the Ma and Pa, someone who actually cares about service and consistent food quality directing employees, managing.

It's not just important to have a "Big Name Franchise" anymore. Isn't this quality of service what you want when you go out? Of course it is!

Our school was designed to show you the actual workings of a successful small town pizzeria first opened in 1993, from dough making to bookkeeping and everything in between. By the way, we offered pasta, ribs, crab cakes and more…not just pizza, something for everyone!

Our first pizzeria, opened in Mendocino County, California and cost about $10,000.00, this included equipment like an oven, prep table and mixer.

In later years we expanded another 600 sq. feet and opened "Ship Wrecked" a bar with Sake Martini's, Sake Margaritas and of course beer and regional wine for a cost of about $12,000.00.

The view from our deck is the beautiful Pacific Ocean. We were in "Wine Country" and on the ocean!

OK, who are or were we? Well to start with at one time we were 5 pizzerias strong and well on the way to starting a franchise or chain.
The units were in small and medium size cities. They ranged in size from 600 square feet to 3000 square feet. We were called Simply Delicious Pizza.

The cost of opening our units varied from "0" to $15,000.00, really. It's easy to spend money, but you don't always need or want to. They were closed or sold when we moved to Florida.

We took over Cosmic Pizza, our first Simply Delicious Pizza location, when we relocated to California and changed its menu as shown later on in this book. (My sister and niece bought our first unit and changed the name when we continued to expand under Simply Delicious. This was that unit).
Cosmic Pizza was unique, both in location as well as menu. Even our layout was unusual. It was made up of a deck overlooking an active but small fishing port, the inside section, looking out at the port, is for families and young people. The inside bar area was separated from the dining area. It was a small pub, very private, with a unique design named, "Shipwrecked".

The design for "Shipwrecked" was inspired from an 1890's, two masted schooners mid-ship design. These tall ships carried timber to southern ports. Of course with a name like "Shipwrecked", the hull, as you can imagine, was upside down!

We were located in northern California, near Sea Ranch and Gualala, on the coast, in the small city of Pt. Arena, population 440. The restaurant was located in the wine country of Mendocino and next door to Alexander Valley, Napa and Sonoma. A wonderful Tourist and resort area.

If we can make it here, in a small city with a population of 440 people what do you think your chances are in a more populated area? That's right... very good!

Our dough was unique as it's a combination of my New York background and sour dough, a la San Francisco. It was the basis of our continued success. We bought our Sour Dough Starter from Old California Sour Dough near San Francisco, Ca. and so should you! Wonderful people!
Our menu recipes, cooking methods and serving techniques were or would have been disclosed during our training.

The Two-Day Training Seminar was made up of four sections. Attendance was limited to 5 Couples per seminar, 10 individuals or 5 couples, or any combination thereof. Pre enrollment was a must. We trained as few as 2 people. We charged only $500 per couple.

Day 1- Morning

Section 1- "the numbers", let's face it, it's all about numbers. If the numbers are not going to provide the return you want then this business is not for you and yours. Return on Investment needed to be discussed.
We started with numbers from formulas that breaks down all expenses you need to know. Also you learned something about food cost and menu plating, pricing.

In addition we covered the cost of equipment at start up. How big do you want to be, what's your dream and what's your budget? Will you borrow, have partners, or build out of pocket. Where do you see your store or stores located?

Will you grow slowly or plan a roll out right away, (this is the reality check section where dreams and financing are looked at from a risk reward basis).

Lunch Break- Informal conversation with your questions and answers from your hosts

Day 1 -Afternoon

Section 2- From flour to pizza, pasta, and more... being a chef is many things and in this section we cover how you create your menu, which will determine the equipment needed as well as the setup of your line and training of your crew.

The menu also determines the cost of plating and ultimately your profit margins. Where you place an item on the menu also is important and is covered as well.

Everything we do actually represents a budget number.
In this section we present you with some basic tools we use with cost or pricing computer programs made using Spread Sheets to help you understand our menu item selections.

Think of this business as a mini manufacturing facility. Once you realize this everything falls into place. It matters not, if you make Pizza or Hamburgers and French fries, the principles are the same.

Evening Assignment- Develop what specific questions you may want covered tomorrow based on today's training

Day 2 - Morning

Section 3- Review of questions coming from evening assignment.

Section 4- We presented some of the alternatives to franchises, sources of food supply, equipment, a general guide to codes and food handling as well as training techniques.

This training was done in a working restaurant and was hands on.

Please consider getting a job at a restaurant similar to the one you're thinking about opening. You'll learn hands on and really see if this is what you want to do!
Recently, I went on line and looked at franchises for pizza, take and bake pizza, and other food franchises... I was shocked at the cost. Especially since I know what equipment costs and how easy it is to train people in the principals of pizzeria or food industry management.

As with all things, "Knowledge" dictates a price and only a fool would tell you that you can go from programming software to making a living as a restaurant owner without help.

Franchising companies do guide and train you and your staff.

Following this section you will find Cosmic Pizzas menu then the Cosmic Pizza and Simply Delicious Pizza recipes.

(The recipe books are still available separately should anyone wish to purchase them as a Kindle or Paper backs.)

The Spread Sheet Management Tools come next and following that our last restaurant, The Chocolate Martini Restaurant and Bar, menu and recipes with Trip Advisor comments.

Look up Pizza Today Magazine on the internet. It's a trade magazine and you will learn a lot from it!

Spread Sheet Management Tools

The following examples of our spread sheet management tools were used daily by us to help control our business.

The Food Cost Generator was basically a tool where we broke down the per pound cost of an ingredient to a 1 ounce cost and then used the spread sheet to total the food cost per item we sold.

Anytime we received a price increase we would enter the price and automatically see if we needed to change our selling price.

We then used a 5 times cost to establish a base selling price when possible. (It depended on competitors pricing for a similar item.)

With the menu and recipes enclosed figuring your own restaurant plating cost is a breeze!

We have expanded this addition by adding other spread sheets we used to operate our business.

These spread sheets will help guide you as to the type of records needed to control costs and business in general.

Some of the forms are from 2003 or 2004. Some are from 1997.

BUDGET VS. ACTUAL MANAGEMENT REPORT- 2003
LOCATION-   Pt Arena

Projected	Monthly	Daily	
Sales	$12,370.00	$562.27	
Less TAX	$896.83	$29.89	
After Tax$	$11,473.18	$382.44	

O/H	Monthly	Daily	
RENT	$1,400.00	$46.67	
Triple Net	$600.00	$20.00	
Office	$750.00	$25.00	
GAS/EL	$600.00	$20.00	
INSC	$200.00	$6.67	
ADV-1.5%	$172.10	$5.74	
TELE	$250.00	$8.33	
AUTO	$350.00	$11.67	
SUB-TOT	$4,322.10	$144.07	37.67%
Food	$2,868.29	$95.61	25.00%
Loan	$1,037.00	$34.57	9.04%
Build out	$0.00	$0.00	0.00%
SUB-TOT	$8,227.39	$274.25	71.71%
GROSS	PROFIT		
SUB-TOT	$3,245.78		

OWNERS DRAW

Monthly	Daily	Bi-Wkly	Daily	Monthly
$2,294.64	$76.49	$1,147.32	20.00%	20.00%

MONTHLY PROFIT	$951.15	8.29%

SUMMARY

Monthly		
	DAILY AVG SALES	$382.44
	MINUS DAILY O/H	$144.07
	MINUS FOOD COST	$95.61
	SUB-TOT	$239.68
	MINUS Draw	$76.49
	SUB -TOT	$316.17

AVG DAILY PROFIT	$66.27

Hourly		
	Sales	$34.77
	OH	$13.10
	Food	$8.69
	Draw	$6.95
	Total Hourly Cost	$28.74
	Hourly Profit	$6.02

Let's take a quick look at this budget and review the numbers under the overhead and food section which was set up for an accountant who we hired for our corporation.

Take out the following; Triple Net, Office, Insurance, Tele, Auto and Loans as business costs. The total of $2150.00 came right to my wife and me paying for our personal expenses. We charged the business for expenses we incurred on behalf of the business and were reimbursed.

Food Cost Generator

Here is how we figured our cost of plating. Under dough you will see a 9oz dough ball and 12oz dough showing a total cost of $0.32 and $0.42 respectively which was derived from the combining of Flour, Sour Dough Starter, Olive Oil, and Butter costs below.

Once you add the section for sauce and cheese you find the heading Basic Pizza Cost and the 5 times calculation for selling price. We always priced pizza with boxes so that we could give the boxes away if people wanted one.

COST STUDY-1/1/03

INGREDIENTS

DOUGH	FLOUR	SOUR/YT	OLIVE OIL	BUTTER	TOTAL
CASE	$12.69	$115.00	$11.26	$77.52	
BATCH	$4.06	$8.21	$0.75	$0.65	$13.67
9OZ	$0.14	$0.14	$0.01	$0.02	$0.32
12OZ	$0.19	$0.19	$0.02	$0.02	$0.42

SAUCE	Pizza letto	FULL	PICANTE	GARLIC	BASIL
CASE	$20.02	$0.00	$0.00	$6.58	$18.24
1 Oz	$0.03	$0.00	$0.00	$0.01	$0.01
2 Oz	$0.06	$0.00	$0.00	$0.02	$0.02
3 Oz	$0.09	$0.00	$0.00	$0.03	$0.04
4 Oz	$0.12	$0.00	$0.00	$0.03	$0.05

CHEESE	30#	1#
CASE	$97.49	$3.25
1/2 Oz	$0.10	
1 Oz	$0.20	
2 Oz	$0.41	

3 Oz	$0.61			
4 Oz	$0.81			
5 Oz	$1.02			
6 Oz	$1.22			
7 Oz	$1.42			

BASIC PIZZA COST

	10"	12"	14"	16"
Dough	$0.32	$0.42	$0.63	$0.83
Sauce	$0.10	$0.15	$0.21	$0.21
Cheese	$0.71	$0.91	$1.12	$1.52
Top Cheese	$0.20	$0.20	$0.20	$0.20
TOTAL	$1.33	$1.69	$2.16	$2.76
Min x 5	$6.66	$8.44	$10.79	$13.82
Current Sell Price	$9.00	$11.00	$14.00	$16.00
Difference +	$2.34	$2.56	$3.21	$2.18
Boxes	$0.23	$0.23	$0.29	$0.35
Insert $20.60	$0.08	$0.08	$0.08	$0.08
5x + Boxed Min	$6.97	$8.75	$11.16	$14.25
(Current Sell Price	$9.00	$11.00	$14.00	$16.00)

The same principal applies for toppings as show by the example below

TOPPINGS

	1#	1 Oz	Portion Small	Med	Large	EX-Larg
Pepperoni	$2.25	$0.14	$0.32	$0.39	$0.49	$0.56
Sausage	$1.80	$0.11	$0.22	$0.36	$0.45	$0.45

Combining the Basic cost with Toppings gives us the following

Cost | Selling

	10 inch	12 inch	14 inch	16 inch	10 inch	12 inch
Cheese Pz	$1.36	$1.72	$2.21	$2.82	$6.79	$8.62
Pepperoni	$1.67	$2.11	$2.70	$3.38	$8.37	$10.56
Sausage	$1.58	$2.09	$2.66	$3.27	$7.91	$10.44

Sales Projection on a monthly basis is necessary for planning of staff needs as well as inventory. As you can see below business grew during Tourist season and declined afterwards.

My projections were sometime wrong but we still grew.

2003	Sales	%of Tot	Projected	%of Tot	$Difference
Jan	$10,146.87	7.27%	$10,146.87	5.91%	$0.00
Feb	$15,005.16	7.17%	$15,005.16	5.83%	$0.00
Mar	$15,143.24	7.27%	$15,143.24	5.91%	$0.00
Apr	$10,688.75	7.66%	$10,688.75	6.23%	$0.00
May	$11,828.62	8.48%	$11,828.62	6.89%	$0.00
Jun	$22,541.68	8.99%	$27,091.52	9.96%	-$4,549.84
July	$24,115.94	10.12%	$31,157.94	12.33%	-$7,042.00
Aug	$28,815.91	13.49%	$36,306.34	15.33%	-$7,490.43
Sept	$21,921.06	8.55%	$16,138.70	9.41%	$4,217.64
Oct	$23,631.28	9.77%	$17,715.92	10.33%	$4,084.64
Nov	$8,384.51	6.01%	$11,488.02	6.70%	$3,103.51
Dec	$7,252.88	5.20%	$8,870.11	5.17%	$1,617.23
Total	$199,476	100%	$211,581	100%	$12,105

While this type of projecting isn't science it can give you a bit of a road map to how your next year will go. It helps you plan you labor needs and inventory levels. Everything works together!

www.ingramcontent.com/pod-product-compliance
Lightning Source LLC
Chambersburg PA
CBHW071548170526
45166CB00004B/1580